MY PURPOSE - SERIES

I0540539

Who am I?

Assisting professionals
regaining
inner joy and peace

EUNICE ANITA

The Netherlands

Who am I?
MY PURPOSE – SERIES
Copyright © 2019 Eunice Anita
Published by Highly Favored Publishing
www.highlyfavored.nl

Editing by Duvilène Pieter
Cover illustration © 2019 Highly Favored Publishing
Book Layout © 2019 Highly Favored Publishing

Complete Jewish Bible (CJB) by David H. Stern. Copyright © 1998. All
rights reserved. Used by permission of Messianic Jewish Publishers, 6120
Day Long Lane, Clarksville, MD 21029. www.messianicjewish.net.

Holy Bible, New International Version®, NIV® Copyright ©1973, 1978,
1984, 2011 by Biblica, Inc.® Used by permission.

Motivational
Paperback ISBN 9789492266-14-9
E-Book Epub ISBN 9789492266-15-6
BISAC REL012090, SEL016000
NUR 707, 740

*Because of the dynamic nature of the Internet, any web addresses or links
contained in this book may have changed since publication and may no
longer be valid.*

*All rights reserved. No part of this publication may be reproduced, distrib-
uted or transmitted in copies, photocopy, microfilm, audio tape or by any
means, without prior written permission of the publisher.*

Contents

Introduction

Ever wondered for real who you are? I have had seasons in which I had asked myself that question.

Questions as, who am I on a professional level, in the church, in the society and why I am whom I am started to ponder in my mind.

We all have a purpose in life. The point is to discover that and experience freedom, sense of accomplishment, and fulfillment on the inside and the outside.

I realized that fulfillment on the outside is *what we show to others and like to think about ourselves* and that the satisfaction on the inside is far more important for *it gives us the balance we need in order to be able to function well till the day we are called to eternal life*.

Why are there in this world so many people that are angry, bitter, burn-out, pressured, feeling that they have failed, or it is just not enough?

There is a great chance that it is due to a lack of inner fulfillment.

I am not a doctor or psychologist and do not pretend to be one either. I just know that the Creator of all, the Almighty God, has a perfect plan for every person and the bad things won't last forever. Difficulties and trials may come, but at last, the victory is in our hands for Christ has already conquered all for us.

Based on the principles mentioned above and concepts of the Bible, I started to meditate on my initial question. The outcome was this booklet filled with questions for you to answer, but also encouraging thoughts, motivation and prayer for the professional that is going thru some hard times and for those that are performing an inner search or want to take control of the process of ensuring not going overboard mentally.

Each chapter opens with a series of thoughts, which can be identified by the *italic* font. Many will be able to recognize themselves, either partially or entirely, in the text as presented. These texts are not to discourage you. They are intended to help you face the reality in which you live or that which you see others are in, and that you could end up in too. Be encouraged because there is a solution to everything.

Before continuing reading, ask the question, *who am I?*

Affirming statements

I am a professional who wants to contribute to the economy, humanity, industry, science, and society; but above all,

\# I realize and admit that I need inner fulfillment as much as all other things that I value in life.

\# My spirit and my soul require refreshment that only the Source of creation can provide.

\# My physical body needs proper nourishment and rest.

\# I am as talented as God has made me capable of.

\# I excel in all I do by the grace of God.

\# I am wonderfully made in the image and likeness of God.

My Inner man

My inner man, who are you? How is it with you? Who is taking care of you?

The journey called life can be tough, but together, we can make it. Surely, we will need assistance. Whom can we ask?

Inner man is described as a person's mind, nature, or soul.[1] Surely, we all have one. We use it regularly, but do we take care of our inner man? If we do, are we doing it the right way? When a car breaks down, we take it to a car dealer or a mechanic. When they cannot resolve the issue, the factory itself is consulted. Sometimes the owner of the car persists for contacting the factory. Shortly said, the maker of the product is contacted. Do we consult our Maker when His product needs revision? Do we persist in reaching Him who knows us from inside out?

---

[1] https://www.collinsdictionary.com/dictionary/english/inner-man

Prayer

Lord, thank You for creating me according to Your image and likeness. You know me better than anyone. You have given me free will. Jesus, I invite You into my life. I ask You to walk with me every day, wherever I go. When my inner man needs a revision, alert me, and teach me how to approach You for this matter. I want, and I will feed myself with food that strengthens me to eternal life. I ask You to help me to digest this food in my mind, heart, and soul, so I may know that all is processed in the right proportion and way. This is my prayer in Jesus' Name, Amen.

Scriptures

Genesis 1:26; Matthew 4:4; John 4:34; John 6:27

I am chosen

Indeed, I am chosen. Not because people are telling me so, but because my Father in Heaven has engraved these words on my heart.

My soul knows it and longs to walk in the path the Father is silently showing to him through my spirit, which is in communion with the Holy Spirit. Why is it then that I feel so empty inside? I look around and realize that I have everything a person can ask for, and still, there is an emptiness inside.

Oh, my soul. What is it that you need? Please help me find the way to the Father, so this void inside can be taken care of. Life can be so more meaningful. I long for the Father to show me this.

What am I chosen for? I am still asking myself.

When we hear the words chosen by God, we tend to think only of serving as Pastors or one of the other Fivefold Ministries.

Child of God, you have been chosen to excel in the area you have been anointed for. It might be business, art, music, caretaker of the elderly, guiding children or students with studies or sports; you name it. Feel the fulfillment of doing that which you are called for, that which bubbles up from inside. It is an outpouring of the love of God, which is channeled through you in order to reach others. Go and complete your missions.

Prayer

Lord, thank You for choosing me before the foundation of the world and setting me in the light. I invite You to be by my side and help me to discover and understand the time of every purpose for which You have called me, and above all to complete them with Your help. I embrace the challenges I may encounter for You have equipped me to overcome them. Thank You, Jesus, for interceding for me. Holy Spirit thank You for helping me out in all the phases of the missions. In Jesus' Name, amen.

Scriptures

Ecclesiastes 3:1; John 15:16; Ephesians 1:4; 1 Peter 2:9

What others think of me

Often, I dedicate effort and time to think about what others may think of me. I tend to do things, not because I like or want to, but because of what others may believe and value. Have I ever taken time to ask myself, is this really what I want or need? Is this what God wants me to do?

The society demands a lot from us, and it is good to think and act outside of one's comfort zone. The problem starts as one starts to live a life based on the preferences and quirks of others. It is easy to put a yoke on a person, and it is oh, so challenging to get rid of those false yokes.

We are all different, and there is a purpose for that. We are to balance out or complement each other and avoid massive cumulation of the same mistakes. Wouldn't it be exciting to think about what is the Lord's opinion about our actions and thoughts?

Prayer

I realize and admit that I was looking for affirmation and approval of men and the moments I had not received that; it became a setback for me. Lord, I give You access to my life. I invite You to come and help me in the process of letting go of the need for getting an approval of men to satisfy my inner man. Teach me to look for and love the approval coming from You on all matters, and also to accept correction.

Help me to understand that the approval of men is to assist in the process of keeping earthly things running in order and that the glory comes only from You. I cry out to You to heal me in my soul for the wounds that are still open / might be open due to experienced negligence by others because of approvals, which I had expected and not received. I pray in Jesus' Name, amen.

Scriptures

Proverbs 29:25; Galatians 1:10

My joyful life

When is it that I have achieved a joyful life?

- *When I can show off with all I have bought with the money I have earned?*
- *When I can compete with others and be better than them on all levels?*
- *Or maybe when I am essential to many people and have many followers?*

When is it that I have reached the life that satisfies my inner man? What kind of life is the one that makes me smile when I am lying in my bed with the lights turned off and thinking of the next day?

Definitely, it is not the one that makes you cry when no one sees you. Don't get it wrong. We need to cry out at times to release our emotions, the good ones, and the sad ones. Here the reference is made to the kind of cry that you want no one to know about. A sadness that suddenly pops up and has become or is getting structural. If you are in that situation, it is time to go back to the basics.

It is time to ask (again): *What is my purpose in life? Where am I standing now in life? Where should I be, not based on what people say but on what God says about me?*

Prayer

Lord, I invite You to be part of my life and to guide me on my walk through life. Thank you for creating me with a purpose. Thank You for revealing and confirming Your purpose for my life to me. I am grateful for the privilege of seeing and enjoying all that You have created. Whenever I want to give up or and tend to forget the purpose, You have given to me, help me to remember that even though I may pass through the valley of the shadow of death, You are at my side. You are my redeemer and my rock. I can experience all the good things of life in, through, and with Jesus. I pray in Jesus' Name. Amen.

Scriptures

Psalms 138:8; Romans 8:28

Peace in my mind

Peace is a term that is often used in conversations and sermons. I hear of it all the time, but what does it mean for me, myself and I?

Peace is described as freedom from disturbance, tranquility, and/or being emotionally or mentally calm.[2]

When can someone say that he/she has peace? Do we all experience peace in the same way? When do I feel and experience peace? A lot of questions. It is essential that you can answer these questions about yourself. Each person is responsible for his/her peace. Sometimes, this requires you to stand up for yourself. You don't have to be rude, just indicate where the boundaries lie. Please don't wait till it is too late.

---

[2] https://en.oxforddictionaries.com/definition/peace

Prayer

Lord, thank You for allowing me to experience peace. Even though it might be a long time ago when I had really experienced a deep sense of peace, I acknowledge that it was a good feeling and that I long to experience it again. Jesus, I invite You to be in my life and to help me regain the peace that only You can provide in my heart. Help me to seek Your peace and keep pursuing it. Assist me in living out of the position of Your peace daily.

Lord, I invite You to stay at my side and to help me work from a stand of peace. I pray in Jesus' Name. Amen.

Scriptures

Isaiah 26:3; Philippians 4:7; Colossians 3:15

My knowledge and skills

Knowledge and skills are unquestionably necessary for development. Where had mine actually come from, and what are they really intended for? It is hard to believe that they are meant for me to destroy myself with.

Below an excerpt from chapter 5 of the book *Stories to tell to show His Greatness*.[3]

***

"Your skills can be cut, molded, and polished throughout courses, experiences, or study. But for this to happen, the skills must have been deposited in you.
Where did all your skills come from?

The natural leaders today are so busy with the quantity and quality of information that they receive that the time to listen to the voice of Adonai has vanished. There is so much to do that the time for communion with the Holy Spirit is simply forgotten. The business might not go as

---

[3] Stories to tell to show His Greatness, God working thru the highly educated, Eunice Anita, AuthorHouse UK, March 2015

well as it used in the past. The customers are leaving, or costs are increasing. There are a lot of circumstances and situations in the professional life for which we are looking for the answers. Where do we find all the answers?

Maybe in new models or structures that will come forth from new ideas, but how do you come up with these? What is the driving force for new plans? Adonai has equipped the highly educated with several gifts. For the use of those gifts in all of their strength, a communion with the Holy Spirit is vital."

Take a moment to think about or analyze what you have read above in context with your own life.

Would it not be wise to take time and acknowledge that your knowledge and skills are meant for the good and not to destroy you?

Would you take time to thank He Who created you for the blessings you have received?

Prayer

Lord, thank You for blessing me with wisdom and the capability of studying and understanding concepts and theories. I invite You to be by my side and to assist me in using all of this while applying good judgment for the fulfillment of my purpose in life. I trust Your commands. Jesus, I invite You to direct me on my journey of achieving inner fulfillment and satisfaction. This is my prayer in Jesus' Name, Amen.

Scriptures

Exodus 31:3; Proverbs 1:7; Proverbs 2:6

My time to rest

The Creator of all rested on the seventh day. Why can't I take time to relax? REAL TIME TO REST. No phone, no computer, let's say no electronics.

Take time to rest your spirit, soul, and body. You will be amazed by the effect that this will have on your inner man.

Oh, and in case your mind tries to trick you and make you feel guilty of putting work aside for a while, remind yourself of this: *when I die, everything will go on as if I have never been there.*

Be a good employee, strive to perform, but do take good care of yourself. Resting is not only sleeping though it is an integral part of it.

Prayer

Lord, thank You for taking care of me even when I am not doing so. You told me to come to You for You will give me rest in my soul. I realize that it is vital for me to give time to my body, soul, and spirit to rest and recharge. Thank You for helping me perform, and also relax. I invite You to assist me day in and day out to keep a balance in all that I do. Please help me to keep all aspects of life in balance. I pray in Jesus' Name, Amen.

Scriptures

Exodus 33:14; Psalm 4:8; Matthew 11:28

I am (not) replaceable

As an employee, employer, advisor, consultant, salesman, neighbor, and so forth, I am replaceable. Another person can take my place and satisfy the need that is present.

As a father, mother, son, daughter, or friend, I am not replaceable!

The loss of a dear one, not only in terms of death but also when not being part of someone's daily life, causes a void in one's heart, which only the Lord can fill up.

The professional in you is satisfied when you are performing at the office, and your work is being valued and recognized. Your inner man is happy when it is loved. Balance is needed in the way you spend your time.

Prayer

Lord, You are the One who has given me the capabilities to be a professional. Thank you that I can function as an employee or employer. Lord, thank You for blessing me with divine health, so I can eat, drink and enjoy the good results of my work.

Lord, I am grateful that I can give and receive the kind of love that is kind, patient, not jealous, not proud, not self-seeking, not easily angered or does not keep a record of wrongs.

I invite You, Jesus, to help me discern the time and to direct my efforts towards that which is suited for the time as indicated by the Father. This is my prayer in Jesus' Name, Amen.

Scriptures

Ecclesiastes 3:1; 9-11 and 22; John 15:13; Ephesians 4:6

I am a trendsetter

What can and should I do to feel and be happy in my inner man, my soul? Am I capable of effecting changes in my life to achieve the aforementioned?

Changing habits requires becoming a trendsetter — not one that influences the whole world, but one that starts with oneself. Everything starts small. If it is a part of your purpose in life to influence a broader group, that will come along the way.

No one can change your life for you. You must act. Be strong and courageous. Be a trendsetter in indicating boundaries, your boundaries for all areas of life. As we are all unique, our limits do vary.

Sometimes the Lord shows you that change is needed and that He will help you. Just remember, His timing is not your timing. Do not get in despair if things are changing at a slower pace or in another way than you had expected. The Lord is not slow in keeping His promises.

He is rather patient with you and maybe waiting for you to repent so He can act and fulfill what He has promised you.

Be a trendsetter in thanking God, even when you do not understand it all yet, for all He has done, is doing and will be doing for you.

Prayer

Lord, You told me not to be conformed to this world, but to be transformed by the renewal of my mind. Jesus, I invite You into my life and ask You to help me with the process of setting new trends that do line up with the perfect will of God. I believe Lord that Your plans for me are to give me a future and hope.

Jesus, help me in my walk to keep going forward and not fall back into old habits that are not conformed to Your will for my life. I pray in Jesus' Name. Amen.

Scriptures

Romans 12:2; Jeremiah 29:11; 2 Peter 3:9

My notes

These are the ideas, prayers, thoughts, or that which came up in my mind when going through this booklet. I will use them to encourage myself and keep my inner man healthy.

_____

_____

_____

_____

_____

_____

_____

_____

_____

_____

_____

_____

About the author

Eunice is a professional with a master's degree in Accounting and Post-Master education in Auditing. After almost one-and-a-half decade of working in the auditing and business sector and having gained leadership experience in the corporate world, she took a leap of faith and started walking on two new roads, the road of entrepreneurship and spiritual growth. The latter required of her to take several steps of faith, leading to a balanced and matured perspective on life, application of Biblical principles, the rationality of science, and the combination of all together. As part of this process, she rolled into a leadership role in a congregational context. She is a professional that believes in the value of knowledge and skills as well as the importance of integrity, morality, sincerity, and unity. Knowledge sharing and helping others grow in their divine given purpose are also important to her. This is why she dedicates time to coaching

and teaching on leadership, financial management, and organizational management blended with relevant principles as described in the Bible.

She is the author of the book *Stories to tell to show His Greatness*, with the subtitle *God working thru the highly educated*. Furthermore, she served as editor of several manuscripts, including academic articles and thesis.

Other publications

Other booklets in the MY PURPOSE - series

Can I achieve more in life?
Assisting man and woman rediscover their purpose in life
Paperback ISBN 978-94-92266-16-3
E-Book Epub ISBN 978-94-92266-17-0

What kind of leader am I?
Assisting leaders in rediscovering how leadership is meant to be
Paperback ISBN 978-94-92266-18-7
E-Book Epub ISBN 978-94-92266-19-4

Other publications of the author

Stories to tell to show His Greatness
God working thru the highly educated
Paperback ISBN 978-15-04937-17-7
E-Book Epub ISBN 978-15-04937-18-4
Published by Authorhouse UK

www.ingramcontent.com/pod-product-compliance
Lightning Source LLC
Chambersburg PA
CBHW061722120626
46550CB00003B/1322